Microwave Dessert Cookbook That You Will Find Helpful

The Ultimate Microwave Dessert Cookbook for Everyone

BY: Allie Allen

COOK & ENJOY

Copyright 2019 Allie Allen

Copyright Notes

This book is written as an informational tool. While the author has taken every precaution to ensure the accuracy of the information provided therein, the reader is warned that they assume all risk when following the content. The author will not be held responsible for any damages that may occur as a result of the readers' actions.

The author does not give permission to reproduce this book in any form, including but not limited to: print, social media posts, electronic copies or photocopies, unless permission is expressly given in writing.

Table of Contents

Delicious Microwave Dessert Recipes 5

1) Healthy Baked Apples 6

2) Traditional Bread Pudding 8

3) Delicious Maple Fudge 10

4) Classic Rice Krispies Treats 12

5) Microwave Style Pecan Brittle 14

6) Classic Fondue 16

7) Microwave Style Cheesecake 18

8) Easy Apple and Blueberry Crunch ... 20

9) Dripping Caramel Popcorn 23

10) Holiday Eggnog Pie 25

11) Microwave Style Cake 28

12) White Chocolate Smothered Grapes 30

13) Decadent Chocolate Pie 32

14) Bark Style Cherry Pistachio Treats 35

15) Creamy Raisin Bread Pudding 37

16) Traditional Rocky Road Candy 39

17) Sweet Sponge Pudding 41

18) Fresh Blueberry Crumble 43

19) Tasty Apple Crisp 45

20) Tasty Cherrio Treats 47

21) Mississippi Style Mud Cake 49

22) Tasty Oatmeal Cookies 52

23) Decadent Hot Fudge Peanut Butter Pudding 54

24) Mouthwatering Fudge 57

25) Tasty Raisins Covered In Chocolate 59

About the Author 61

Author's Afterthoughts 63

Delicious Microwave Dessert Recipes

sssssssssssssssssssssssssssssssssssssssssssssss

1) Healthy Baked Apples

While apples are certainly good on their own, you haven't lived until your have enjoyed one of these bad boys. Incredibly easy to make and great taste, this is one recipe that you will want to make again and again.

Serving Sizes: 3 Apples

Cooking Time: 15 Minutes

List of Ingredients:

- 3 Apples, Large
- 1 tablespoon of Raisins
- 3 Tablespoons of Brown Sugar, Granulated
- 1 teaspoon of Cinnamon, Ground
- 1 tablespoon Butter
- ¾ Cup of Water, Warm
- ¾ Cup of Ice Cream, Vanilla Flavored

ssssssssssssssssssssssssssssssssssssssssssssssss

Procedure:

1. The first thing you will want to do is core your apples and peel the top half of an inch of it. Then fill up your cores with all of your remaining ingredients and pack it well by using your thumb.

2. Then fill the bottom of a medium sized microwave safe dish with some water and place your apples into the dish, with the stuffed side facing up.

3. Cover your dish with some plastic wrap and pierce the top to let it breathe. Place the apples into your microwave and microwave on the highest setting for the next 5 to 6 minutes.

4. Remove your apples and serve them topped with some ice cream. Serve immediately and enjoy.

2) Traditional Bread Pudding

If you are looking for a traditional and great tasting dessert to serve, this is the perfect recipe for you. This is a great recipe to serve during the holidays or whenever you want to serve something special.

Serving Sizes: 6 Servings

Cooking Time: 25 Minutes

List of Ingredients:

- 4 Cups of Bread, Lightly Packed and Cut Into Small Cubes
- ½ Cup of Brown Sugar, Packed
- ¼ teaspoons of Salt
- ½ Cup of Raisins
- 2 Cups of Milk, Whole
- ¼ Cup of Butter, Melted
- 2 Eggs, Large In Size and Beaten

sssssssssssssssssssssssssssssssssssssssssssss

Procedure:

1. Take your bread cubes and spread them evenly in a medium sized round microwave safe dish. Then sprinkle your raisins, sugar and salt on top.

2. Place your whole milk into a measuring cup and add your butter. Place into your microwave and microwave on the highest setting for 4 minutes or until the butter is fully melted and your milk is warm.

3. Using a small bowl roughly whisk your eggs and combine it well with your butter and milk. Pour this mixture over your bread.

4. Place your dish into your microwave and microwave on the highest setting for the next 9 to 12 minutes.

5. Once your dish is fully cooked you may notice that it is still slightly soft. This is normal and well set once the pudding fully cools. Serve warm or to whatever your preference may be.

3) Delicious Maple Fudge

While fudge itself tastes incredible, it really could not get any better than when you add the sweet and rich taste of maple to it. This is one fudge recipe that you are going to drool over.

Serving Sizes: 6 Servings

Cooking Time: 10 Minutes

List of Ingredients:

- 1 Package of Sugar, Confectioners
- 3 Tablespoons of Milk, Whole
- 1 tablespoon of Maple Extract
- ½ Cup of Butter
- ¾ Cup of Walnuts, Roughly Chopped

sssssssssssssssssssssssssssssssssssssssssss

Procedure:

1. The first thing that you will want to do is line a medium sized baking dish with some plastic wrap.

2. Then sift your confectioner's sugar into a large sized bowl that is microwave safe. Add in the rest of your ingredients except for your walnuts into the bowl. Make sure that you do not stir the mixture. Leave it as is.

3. Place your mixture into your microwave and microwave on high for 3 minutes.

4. Remove from your microwave and stir in your walnuts gently until your fudge begins to thicken. Pour your fudge mixture into your lined baking dish. Make sure that you smooth the top of it with a rubber spatula.

5. Place your fudge into your refrigerator and let it chill for 15 minutes. After 15 minutes remove and cut up your fudge into small squares. Enjoy immediately or store in a container to enjoy later.

4) Classic Rice Krispies Treats

One of the best dessert snacks to make that every child and adult will love is this classic recipe. Just take these on the go to enjoy a great tasting dessert wherever you are.

Serving Sizes: 12 Servings

Cooking Time: 7 Minutes

List of Ingredients:

- 3 Tablespoons of Butter
- 40 Marshmallows, Large In Size
- 6 Cups of Rice Krispies

ssssssssssssssssssssssssssssssssssssssssssss

Procedure:

1. Using a large sized microwave safe bowl, heat up your butter and marshmallows together in your microwave for about 3 minutes. Make sure that after 2 minutes, you give your butter and marshmallow mixture a nice stir. Upon finishing its cooking continue stirring until your mixture is smooth in consistency.

2. Next add in your Rice Krispies cereal and stir until it is evenly coated.

3. Then using a greased up cooking pan, press your mixture into it and let it set. Cut your mixture into even squares the moment they are cool. Serve whenever you are ready to enjoy them.

5) Microwave Style Pecan Brittle

If you are looking for a recipe that is dripping in pecans and that will fill your nutty craving, this is the recipe for you. It is incredibly easy to make and is a dish that you will fall in love with.

Serving Sizes: 1 Serving

Cooking Time: 30 Minutes

List of Ingredients:

- 2 Cup of Sugar, White
- ½ Cup of Corn Syrup, Light
- 1 Cup of Pecan, Roughly Chopped
- 1 teaspoon of Butter or Margarine, Slightly Melted
- 1 teaspoon of Vanilla Extract
- 1 teaspoon of Baking Soda

ssssssssssssssssssssssssssssssssssssssssssss

Procedure:

1. Combine your sugar and corn syrup on a small size bowl that is microwave safe. Stir your ingredients well. Place this into your microwave and microwave on high for the next 4 minutes.

2. After 4 minutes stir in your chopped pecans. Place back into your microwave and microwave on high for the next 5 to 7 minutes or until it is lightly brown in color.

3. Remove from microwave and stir in your melted butter and vanilla until well mixed. Place back into your microwave for 1 minute. Remove and stir in your baking soda until it is foamy in texture.

4. Pour your next mixture into a baking sheet that is lightly greased. Set to cool on a wire rack. Once fully cooled break your brittle into small pieces and serve immediately or store in a container to enjoy later.

6) Classic Fondue

Everybody loves a good 'ole fondue. With this recipe your will be able to dip whatever your heart desires into the fondue, whether it be strawberries, cookies or small cakes. This is one recipe that every chocoholic will drool over.

Serving Sizes: 2 Servings

Cooking Time: 2 Minutes

List of Ingredients:

- ½ Cup of Milk, Whole
- 1 Chocolate Bar, Your Favorite Kind

sssssssssssssssssssssssssssssssssssssssssssss

Procedure:

1. The first thing that you will want to do is pour your milk into a microwave safe bowl and pop it into your microwave to heat up for about a minute and a half.

2. Then add in your chocolate and heat it up once again for another minute.

3. Serve with some fresh apples, strawberries or marshmallows. Enjoy!

7) Microwave Style Cheesecake

Who doesn't love a good cheesecake? With this recipe now you can enjoy a great tasting cheesecake without all of the hassle.

Serving Sizes: 1 Serving

Cooking Time: 2 Minutes

List of Ingredients:

- 2 Ounces of Cream Cheese, Softened
- 2 Tablespoons of Sour Cream, Low Fat
- 1 Egg, Large In Size
- ½ teaspoons of Lemon Juice, Fresh
- ¼ teaspoons of Vanilla
- 2 to 4 Tablespoons of Sugar Substitute

ssssssssssssssssssssssssssssssssssssssssssssss

Procedure:

1. Using a medium sized microwave sized bowl, mix all of your ingredients together until they are thoroughly mixed.

2. Place into your microwave and cook on the highest setting for about 90 seconds. As it cooks make sure that your stir your ingredients every 30 seconds to incorporate all of the ingredients.

3. Remove and place into your refrigerator to chill. Serve and enjoy. For the best results I recommend serving with some fresh fruit and whipped cream.

8) Easy Apple and Blueberry Crunch

Sometimes we all need something tasty and sweet to get through our tough days. This is one of those recipes that you can put together in a snap and take on the go whenever you have to rush out of the house.

Serving Sizes: 8 Servings

Cooking Time: 15 Minutes

List of Ingredients:

- 1 Cup of Flour, All Purpose
- ¾ Cup of Brown Sugar, Packed
- ½ Cup of Oats, Rolled
- ¼ Cup of Graham Crackers, Crumbs Only
- 1 teaspoon of Cinnamon, Ground
- ½ Cup of Butter, Melted
- 3 ½ Cups of Apples, Peeled and Sliced
- 1 ½ Cups of Blueberries, Fresh
- 1 tablespoon of Lemon Juice, Fresh
- ¼ Cup of Sugar, White
- 2 Tablespoons of Cornstarch
- 1 Cup of Water, Cold
- 1 teaspoon of Vanilla Extract

sssssssssssssssssssssssssssssssssssssssssssss

Procedure:

1. The first thing that you will want to do is grease up a medium sized microwave safe casserole dish.

2. Then using a medium sized bowl mix together until thoroughly combined. Place into your microwave and microwave on the highest setting in 45 second intervals, making sure to stir frequently until your sauce is thick in consistency.

3. Then continue cooking for an addition 8 to 10 minutes or until the juices of your fruit are bubbling. Remove and allow it to cool slightly before serving.

9) Dripping Caramel Popcorn

Getting ready to enjoy a good movie? Then what you need to make it even better is some caramel covered popcorn. This is a favorite snack dish that not only tastes amazing, but that will leave you wanting more.

Serving Sizes: 4 Servings

Cooking Time: 10 Minutes

List of Ingredients:

- 2 to 3 Quarts of Popcorn, Freshly Popped
- ½ Cup of Butter, Melted
- 1 Cup of Brown Sugar, Packed
- ¼ Cup of Corn Syrup, Light
- ½ teaspoons of Salt
- ¾ teaspoons of Baking Soda

sssssssssssssssssssssssssssssssssssssssssssss

Procedure:

1. Using a large sized microwave bowl combine your corn syrup, sugar, melted butter and salt together and stir. Place in your microwave and microwave on the highest setting for ½ to 3 minutes until your mixture begins to bubble.

2. Remove from your microwave and mix in your baking soda until thoroughly blended.

3. Next place your popcorn into a paper grocery bag and pour your freshly made caramel over the top and fold your bag. Put into your microwave and cook on high for another minute and 20 seconds. Remove from microwave.

4. Shake your popcorn roughly to evenly coat the popcorn. Once thoroughly coated and pout onto a cooking sheet to cool slightly. Serve while it is still warm.

10) Holiday Eggnog Pie

During the holidays, especially Christmas, one of the most popular beverages to enjoy is eggnog. Now with this recipe you can enjoy eggnog in the form of a pie. Not only will it leave your holiday guests craving for more, but you will want to make it for every holiday season.

Serving Sizes: 1 Pie

Cooking Time: 4 Hours and 10 Minutes

List of Ingredients:

- ¼ Cup of Water, Cold
- 1 Pack of Jello, Unflavored
- 1 Cup of Milk, Whole
- ¾ Cup of Sugar, White
- 2 Eggs, Large In Size and Beaten Lightly
- ¼ Cup of Rum
- 1 Cup of Whipping Cream
- 1 Pie Shell, Fully Baked
- ½ teaspoons of Nutmeg, Ground

ssssssssssssssssssssssssssssssssssssssssssssssss

Procedure:

1. Use a small sized bowl to let your jello dissolve in some water (follow the instructions on the package). Then using a separate microwave safe bowl, combine with your milk and ½ of your sugar. Stir to combine all of the ingredients. Place into your microwave and microwave for 3 minutes or until your milk begins to boil slightly.

2. In a medium sized bowl, stir your jello mixture into your milk mixture. Then gradually mix in your eggs until everything is completely combined. Pop your mixture into your microwave and microwave at 1 minute intervals, making sure to whisk your mixture each minute until it thickens. Remove your mixture from your microwave and pour in your rum next.

3. Place your mixture into your refrigerator until it starts to set, but make sure that you stir it every once in a while as it chills.

4. Then using a medium sized bowl, whip up your whipped cream softly until small peaks begin to form on the surface. Last beat in what is left of your sugar. Set aside half of this to use as a garnish. Keep the remainder refrigerated.

5. Once your filling chills, mix in your whipped cream mixture until evenly combined and pour into your pre-baked pie crust. Cover and set in your refrigerator to chill for 2 to 3 hours.

6. Top with your leftover whipped cream and a dash of nutmeg and enjoy immediately.

11) Microwave Style Cake

Cake is the ultimate go-to dessert recipe. It is not only easy to make, but you can make virtually any style cake that you want. I can assure you that you will fall in love with this recipe.

Serving Sizes: 12 Servings

Cooking Time: 25 Minutes

List of Ingredients:

- 1 Package of Yellow Cake Mix
- 3 Eggs, Large In Size
- 1, 21 Ounce Can of Apple Pie Filling
- ½ Cup of Applesauce, Your Favorite Brand

sssssssssssssssssssssssssssssssssssssssssssss

Procedure:

1. Using a medium sized mixing bowl combine your cake mix, eggs, applesauce and pie filling together until moist in consistency.

2. Then using a bundt cake pan that is microwave safe pour your mixture into the pan.

3. Place your pan into your microwave and cook on high for 6 minutes and 30 seconds. After this time turn your pan and continue cooking for an additional 6 minutes and 30 seconds.

4. Remove from your microwave and cook your pan with a dish. Let your cake stand for the next 5 minutes.

5. Next turn your cake over so that it rests on the dish and serve while still warm.

12) White Chocolate Smothered Grapes

Grapes are a tasty fruit to enjoy all on their own, but you haven't lived until you have tried them smothered in white chocolate. With this recipe you can enjoy a tasty snack that is not only sweet, but that is healthy as well.

Serving Sizes: 20 Servings

Cooking Time: 7 Minutes

List of Ingredients:

- 2 Cups of White Chocolate Chips, Your Favorite Brand
- 2 teaspoons of Shortening
- 1 Pound of Grapes, Seedless
- 1 Cup of Peanuts, Salted and Finely Chopped

sssssssssssssssssssssssssssssssssssssssssssssss

Procedure:

1. Using a medium sized microwave safe bowl, combine your white chocolate chips and shortening together. Place into your microwave and microwave on the highest setting for 30 second intervals, making sure to stir between each interval and until your mixture is fully melted and smooth in consistency.

2. Spread your finely chopped peanuts onto a dinner plate that is covered with a sheet of wax paper.

3. Next you will want to dip freshly washed grapes into your chocolate and then roll them in your chopped peanuts. Set your grapes onto your wax paper to dry. Once they are dried serve and enjoy immediately.

13) Decadent Chocolate Pie

If you are craving chocolate, this recipe is for you. This recipe will make the most sweet tasting and delicious chocolate pie that will taste as if it has just popped out of the oven.

Serving Sizes: 1 Pie

Cooking Time: 25 Minutes

List of Ingredients:

- 1 Pie Shell, Premade and Baked
- ¾ Cup of Sugar, White
- ¼ Cup of Cornstarch
- 1/3 Cup of Cocoa Powder, Unsweetened
- ¼ teaspoons of Salt
- 2 Cups of Milk, Whole
- 3 Eggs, Only The Yolks and Thoroughly Beaten
- 2 Tablespoons of Butter, Melted
- 1 teaspoon of Vanilla Extract
- 3 Eggs, Whites Only and Beaten
- ¼ teaspoons Cream of Tartar

- 6 Tablespoons of Sugar, White
- ½ teaspoons of Vanilla Extract

sssssssssssssssssssssssssssssssssssssssssssssss

Procedure:

1. Preheat your oven to 375 degrees.

2. While your oven is heating up using a medium sized casserole dish that is microwave safe and combine your cocoa powder, salt, whole milk, cornstarch and sugar. Mix until thoroughly mixed together.

3. Place this into your microwave and microwave on the highest setting for the next 5 to 8 minutes or until thick in consistency. Make sure that you stir the mixture at least halfway through the cooking process.

4. Then using a small sized bowl, place a small amount of your hot mixture with your egg yolks. Stir this back into your original mixture. Place this back into your microwave and microwave on the highest setting for the next minute and a half to 2 minutes or until thick in consistency. Make sure that you stir frequently.

Make Meringue:

1. Using a small sized bowl beat your egg whites and cream of tartar together until it is foamy in texture. Then gradually stir in your sugar until stiff peaks begin to form.

2. Then stir in your vanilla extract.

3. Spread your newly made meringue over the top of your pie filling.

4. Seal your pie with some aluminum foil and place into your preheated oven to bake for the next 8 minutes or until the meringue turns brown in color.

14) Bark Style Cherry Pistachio Treats

If you have never heard of this kind of recipe before, don't worry. I didn't hear of it either until I made it for the first time until I made it myself. While the name may sound strange, this is one recipe that you have to try out for yourself.

Serving Sizes: 3 ½ Pounds of Bark

Cooking Time: 1 Hour and 5 Minutes

List of Ingredients:

- 1 ¼ Cup of Cherries, Dried
- 2 Tablespoons of Water
- 2, 11 Ounce Packs of White Chocolate Chips, Your Favorite Brand
- 4, 3 Ounce Bars of Candy Coating, Vanilla Flavored
- 1 ¼ Cups of Pistachio Nuts, Roughly Chopped

sssssssssssssssssssssssssssssssssssssssssssss

Procedure:

1. Using a small sized glass bowl that is microwave safe, pour your cherries into it and microwave your cherries with some water on the highest setting for 2 minutes. After 2 minutes remove your cherries and drain them. Set them aside.

2. Then using a separate medium sized microwave safe bowl, microwave your chocolate chips and vanilla flavored candy coating together until both are completely melted and smooth in consistency. Make sure that you stir your mixture occasionally while it is cooking.

3. Next stir in your cherries and pistachios until well blended. Then spread your mixture onto a pan that is lined with some wax paper. Place it into your refrigerator and chill for 1 hour or until it is firm. Once it is firm slice up your bark into small squares and enjoy whenever you are ready.

15) Creamy Raisin Bread Pudding

If you are looking for a dessert recipe to change up your dessert menu, this is the perfect recipe for you. It only takes a couple of minutes to put together and will leave you craving more.

Serving Sizes: 3 Servings

Cooking Time: 30 Minutes

List of Ingredients:

- 16 Slices of Raisin Bread, Cut Into Small Cubes
- ½ Cup of Sugar, White
- 1/8 teaspoons of Cinnamon, Ground
- 2 Cups of Milk, Whole
- ¼ Cup of Butter, Melted
- 5 Eggs, Roughly Beaten
- ½ Cup of Sugar, White
- 1 teaspoon of Vanilla Extract

sssssssssssssssssssssssssssssssssssssssssssssssss

Procedure:

1. Using a medium sized baking dish that is microwave safe and line it with your raisin bread. Then sprinkle your sugar and cinnamon evenly over your bread. Set this aside.

2. Then place your milk and melted butter in a microwave safe brown and microwave on medium heat for the next 4 ½ to 5 ½ minutes or until your milk is scalding hot. Remove from your microwave and quickly stir in your eggs, sugar and vanilla. Stir until evenly mixed. Pour this mixture over your cubes of bread.

3. Cover your bread with some plastic wrap and microwave on medium heat for the next 17 to 19 minutes or until your pudding is fully set. Remove and allow to cool slightly. Serve and enjoy.

16) Traditional Rocky Road Candy

If you are ever suffering from a bad sweet tooth, this recipe will come to your rescue. This recipe contains just two ingredients so you won't have to wait for long to taste it!

Serving Sizes: 24 Servings

Cooking Time: 2 Hours and 10 Minutes

List of Ingredients:

- 3, 7 Ounce Milk Chocolate Bars, With Almonds
- 1 Cup of Marshmallows, Miniature

sssssssssssssssssssssssssssssssssssssssssssssss

Procedure:

1. The first thing that you will want to do is to place your chocolate bars into a microwave safe bowl or container and pop it into your microwave. Microwave on the lowest setting until the chocolate is completely melted. This should take about 5 minutes or so.

2. Then stir your chocolate and let it cool to the point that it will not melt your marshmallows. Once your chocolate is cool enough stir in your marshmallows and stir until thoroughly blended together.

3. Next pour this mixture into a baking dish and place it into your fridge to chill. This should take about 2 hours. Once it is chilled, break your candy into pieces to serve. Enjoy!

17) Sweet Sponge Pudding

This yet another sweet tasting pudding recipe that you are going to drool over. Sweet to taste and extremely creamy, this is one recipe that you are going to want to make over and over again.

Serving Sizes: 4 Servings

Cooking Time: 10 Minutes

List of Ingredients:

- ½ Cup of Butter
- ¼ Cup of Sugar, White
- ½ Cup of Flour, Self-Rising
- 1 Egg, Roughly Beaten
- 2 Tablespoons of Milk, Whole

sssssssssssssssssssssssssssssssssssssssssssss

Procedure:

1. Use a medium sized bowl and cream together your butter and sugar until smooth in consistency. Then mix in your whole milk and egg gradually. You want to do this to avoid curdling the butter.

2. Sift your flour and fold in your flour gently. Transfer this mixture into a microwave safe bowl.

3. Cover your bowl and cook for 3 ½ minutes in your microwave or until the pudding begins to appear set. The pudding will jiggle and the top of the pudding will be sticky. Remove and serve while it is still hot. Enjoy.

18) Fresh Blueberry Crumble

If you are looking for something that will feed plenty of people, but that will not take you too much time to put together, this is the perfect recipe for you. I recommend using only the freshest ingredients that you can to get the best results.

Serving Sizes: 4 Servings

Cooking Time: 15 Minutes

List of Ingredients:

- 3 Cups of Blueberries, Fresh
- 3 Tablespoons of Sugar, White
- 1 tablespoon of Cornstarch
- 1/3 Cup of Oats, Old Fashioned
- 1/3 Cup of Brown Sugar, Packed
- 3 Tablespoons of Flour
- 2 Tablespoons of Almonds, Freshly Chopped
- ¼ - ½ teaspoons of Cinnamon, Ground
- 3 Tablespoons of Butter, Cold
- Some Vanilla Ice Cream, Optional

sss

Procedure:

1. Using a greased up pie pan, combine your fresh blueberries, cornstarch and sugar together until everything is evenly combined. Place this into your microwave and microwave on the highest setting for the next 7 to 8 minutes or until the mixture is thick in consistency. Make sure that you stir at least twice during the cooking process.

2. Then using a small sized bowl, combine your oats, packed brown sugar, ground cinnamon and chopped almonds together until everything is evenly mixed.

3. Gently cut in your cold butter into your oat mixture until your mixture begins to resemble a crumble. Then sprinkle your oat mixture over your blueberry mixture and pop it into your microwave.

4. Microwave on the highest setting for the next 2 to 3 minutes or until your butter is completely melted. Remove and serve with some ice cream if you wish. Enjoy!

19) Tasty Apple Crisp

Traditionally apple crisp is usually time-consuming to put together. However, with this microwave recipe, you can make delicious apple crisp in just a matter of minutes.

Serving Sizes: 6 Servings

Cooking Time: 12 to 15 Minutes

List of Ingredients:

- 4 Apples, Granny Smith, Large In Size, Peeled, Cored and Sliced
- ½ Cup of Butter, Melted
- ¾ Cup o Brown Sugar, Packed
- ¾ Cup of Oats, Quick Cooking
- ½ Cup of Flour, All Purpose
- 1 teaspoon of Cinnamon, Ground
- ½ teaspoons of Allspice

ssssssssssssssssssssssssssssssssssssssssssssss

Procedure:

1. Using a large sized baking dish that is microwave save, spread your apples evenly over the pan.

2. Then using a medium sized bowl combine the rest of your ingredients until they are thoroughly mixed together. Spread this mixture evenly over the top of your apples.

3. Place your dish in your microwave to cook on the highest setting for the next 10 to 12 minutes or until the apples are tender. Remove and allow to cool slightly. Enjoy.

20) Tasty Cherrio Treats

While you learned how to make delicious Rice Krispies treats earlier, now it is time for you to learn how to make another snack from a breakfast cereal: Cherrios. This is a great recipe to put together for your kids or friends and they will love them all the same

Serving Sizes: 3 Servings

Cooking Time: 10 Minutes

List of Ingredients:

- 3 Tablespoons of Butter, Melted
- 1, 10 Ounce Pack of Marshmallows, Mini
- ½ Cup of Peanut Butter
- 5 Cups of Cheerios Cereal
- 1 Cup of M&M's, Plain or Peanut Butter

ssssssssssssssssssssssssssssssssssssssssssssss

Procedure:

1. Place your butter and your marshmallows together in a large sized microwave safe bowl. Microwave uncovered on the highest setting for the next 2-3 minutes or until your mixture becomes puffy.

2. Then stir in your peanut butter and blend until it is thoroughly mixed. Then add in your cereal and M&M's and stir again until it is mixed well.

3. Next grease up a large sized baking sheet and gently spoon your mixture into the press. Press to flatten it. Allow your mixture to cool completely before cutting it up in small squares. Serve whenever you are ready to enjoy it.

21) Mississippi Style Mud Cake

One of the traditional dishes that everyone must try especially if they are a tourist to the state is the Mississippi Mud Cake. This is every sweet addicts dream come true.

Serving Sizes: 16 Servings

Cooking Time: 35 Minutes

Ingredients for the Cake:

- 1 Cup of Butter
- 2 Cups of Sugar, White
- ½ Cup of Cocoa Powder, Unsweetened
- 4 Eggs, Large In Size
- 2 teaspoons of Vanilla Extract
- 1 ½ Cups of Flour, All Purpose
- ¼ Cup of Walnuts, Coarsely Chopped
- ¼ teaspoons of Salt
- ½ Cup of Marshmallows, Miniature

Ingredients for the Frosting:

- ½ Cup of Butter
- 1/3 Cup of Milk, Whole
- ¼ Cup of Cocoa Powder, Unsweetened
- ½ teaspoons of Vanilla Extract
- 4 Cups of Sugar, Confectioners

sssssssssssssssssssssssssssssssssssssssssssss

Procedure:

For the Cake:

1. Using a large sized mixing bowl, place your butter into it and microwave on the highest setting for 1 to 1 ½ minutes or until the butter is fully melted.

2. Remove from microwave and stir in your sugar and cocoa powder. Then add in your eggs and vanilla. Beat this mixture vigorously until it is well blended. Then stir in your salt, flour and nuts and stir until thoroughly combined. Let your newly made batter rest for the next 10 minutes.

3. After 10 minutes pour your batter into a large sized microwave safe dish. Pop the pan into your microwave and microwave on the medium setting for about 9 minutes, making sure to rotate your dish after 3 minutes of cooking.

4. After this microwave your batter on the highest setting for the next 3 to 5 minutes, making sure that you rotate it halfway through the cooking process or until the top of the cake is mostly dry. Remove from your microwave and sprinkle your marshmallows evenly over the top of your cake. Let your cake stand for the next 5 minutes or until the marshmallows have melted slightly.

For the Frosting:

1. Melt your butter in a large sized bowl. Then stir in your milk, cocoa powder and vanilla.

2. Next add in your confectioners' sugar and beat vigorously until smooth in consistency.

3. Spread your frosting evenly over the top of your marshmallows and let your cake stand for at least 30 minutes or until it is slightly warm in temperature. Serve and enjoy when ready.

22) Tasty Oatmeal Cookies

This is a special recipe for all of the cookie lovers out there. This recipe is incredibly easy to put together and will make you the ultimate cookie chef in your home.

Serving Sizes: 5 Servings

Cooking Time: 7 Minutes

List of Ingredients:

- 2 Cups of Sugar, White
- ¼ Cup of Margarine, Softened
- ½ Cup of Milk, Whole
- ¼ Cup of Cocoa
- 1 teaspoon of Vanilla
- ½ Cup of Peanut Butter, Your Favorite Brand
- 3 Cups of Oats, Quick Preferable

ssssssssssssssssssssssssssssssssssssssssssssss

Procedure:

1. Using a large sized bowl that is microwave safe, mix together all of your ingredients except for your peanut butter and oats and blended until completely mixed together. Pop this mixture into your microwave and microwave on the highest setting for 2 minutes. After 2 minutes give your mixture a quick stir.

2. Then stir in your peanut butter until it is well blended with your mixture. Add in your oats and stir until completely combined. Take out a large spoon and drop a few spoonfuls of your cookie dough onto a baking sheet covered with wax paper. Press to flatten them.

3. Let your cookies cool completely and enjoy whenever you are ready.

23) Decadent Hot Fudge Peanut Butter Pudding

This is a recipe for all of the peanut butter lovers out there. This fudge is extremely rich in flavor and quite easy to put together. This is certainly one recipe that you are going to want to make again and again.

Serving Sizes: 8 Servings

Cooking Time: 15 Minutes

List of Ingredients:

- 1 Cup of Flour, All Purpose
- ¾ Cup of Sugar, White
- ½ Cup of Milk, Whole
- ½ Cup of Peanut Butter, your Favorite Kind
- 2 Tablespoons of Cocoa Powder, Unsweetened
- 2 teaspoons of Vegetable Oil
- 1 teaspoon of Vanilla Extract
- ½ teaspoons of Baking Powder
- ½ teaspoons of Salt
- 1 ¾ Cup of Water, Hot
- 1 Cup of Brown Sugar, packed
- ¼ Cup of Cocoa Powder, Unsweetened

ssssssssssssssssssssssssssssssssssssssssssssss

Procedure:

1. Using a large sized mixing bowl mix your flour, milk, sugar, peanut butter, cocoa powder, vegetable oil, salt, baking powder and vanilla extract together until you have a batter that is smooth in consistency. Spread this batter into a medium sized microwave safe dish.

2. Then using a separate medium sized bowl, combine your water, brown sugar and cocoa powder together until everything is completely dissolved. Pour this mixture over your batter.

3. Place your dish into your microwave and cook for 9 minutes, making sure that you turn your dish halfway through the cooking process. Continue cooking for an additional 6 minutes or until your batter is set.

4. Remove from your microwave and let cool. Serve once you are ready.

24) Mouthwatering Fudge

This recipe is also known as Fantasy Fudge and that is exactly where you will end up upon trying to recipe for yourself. Dripping in decadent chocolate, this is one treat you will certainly want to make over and over again.

Serving Sizes: 6 Servings

Cooking Time: 15 Minutes

List of Ingredients:

- ¾ Cup of Butter, Melted
- 3 Cups of Sugar, White
- 1, 5 Ounce Can of Milk, Evaporated
- 1, 12 Ounce Pack of Chocolate Chips, Semi Sweet
- 1, 7 Ounce Jar of Crème, Marshmallow
- 1 teaspoon of Vanilla
- 1 Cup of Walnuts, Chopped

ssssssssssssssssssssssssssssssssssssssssssssssss

Procedure:

1. Microwave your butter on the highest setting for about 1 minute or until it is fully melted. Then add in your sugar and evaporated milk. Mix until well blended.

2. Microwave your mixture on the highest setting for 5 minutes, making sure that you stir after 3 minutes. Remove your mixture from your microwave and scrape the sides of the bowl clean. Pop back into your microwave and microwave on the highest 5 ½ minutes, making sure to stir after 3 minutes. Let your mixture stand for 2 minutes.

3. Next add in your chocolate chips and stir until everything is evenly blended together. Then add in your marshmallow crème and vanilla, stirring once again to mix everything together. Last add in your chopped nuts and stir to combine.

4. Spread this mixture onto a medium sized baking pan that is greased and let the mixture to cool completely. Once fully cooled cut your fudge into squares and enjoy whenever you are ready.

25) Tasty Raisins Covered In Chocolate

For a simple desert snack that you can pick at whenever your heart contents, this is one of the best and most perfect dishes that you can make. Incredibly tasty and easy to make, this is one dish that you will make as frequently as possible.

Serving Sizes: 4 Servings

Cooking Time: 5 Minutes

List of Ingredients:

- 11 ½ Ounces of Chocolate Chips, Milk Chocolate
- 4 Ounces of White Chocolate
- 9 Ounces of Raisins

sssssssssssssssssssssssssssssssssssssssssssss

Procedure:

1. Place both your milk chocolate chips and white chocolate into a medium sized microwave safe bowl. Place into your microwave and microwave on the highest setting for at least 1 minute. Remove from microwave and stir. Place back into your microwave and microwave for an additional 45 seconds and stir.

2. Add in your raising and stir until evenly coated. Feel free to add in more raisins in your need to. Take your mixture and dollop a few spoonfuls' onto a cookie sheet and allow to cool. Serve once it is completely cool.

About the Author

Allie Allen developed her passion for the culinary arts at the tender age of five when she would help her mother cook for their large family of 8. Even back then, her family knew this would be more than a hobby for the young Allie and when she graduated from high school, she applied to cooking school in London. It had always been a dream of the young chef to study with some of Europe's best and she made it happen by attending the Chef Academy of London.

After graduation, Allie decided to bring her skills back to North America and open up her own restaurant. After 10 successful years as head chef and owner, she decided to sell her business and pursue other career avenues. This monumental decision led Allie to her true calling, teaching. She also started to write e-books for her students to study at home for practice. She is now the proud author of several e-books and gives private and semi-private cooking lessons to a range of students at all levels of experience.

Stay tuned for more from this dynamic chef and teacher when she releases more informative e-books on cooking and baking in the near future. Her work is infused with stores and anecdotes you will love!

Author's Afterthoughts

I can't tell you how grateful I am that you decided to read my book. My most heartfelt thanks that you took time out of your life to choose my work and I hope you find benefit within these pages.

There are so many books available today that offer similar content so that makes it even more humbling that you decided to buying mine.

Tell me what you thought! I am eager to hear your opinion and ideas on what you read as are others who are looking for a good book to buy. Leave a review on Amazon.com so others can benefit from your wisdom!

With much thanks,

Allie Allen

Made in the USA
Monee, IL
03 September 2021